Yes!

I SAID NO!

M000012241

Yes!

I SAID NO!

HOW TO SET HEALTHY

BOUNDARIES AND INCREASE

YOUR SELF ESTEEM

BARBRA E. RUSSELL

**Yes! I Said No! How to Set Healthy Boundaries
and Increase Your Self-Esteem**
Published by Noble House Press
Aurora, CO

Copyright ©2017 Barbra E. Russell. All rights reserved.

No part of this book may be reproduced in any form or by any mechanical means, including information storage and retrieval systems without permission in writing from the publisher/author, except by a reviewer who may quote passages in a review.

All images, logos, quotes, and trademarks included in this book are subject to use according to trademark and copyright laws of the United States of America.

Library of Congress Control Number: 2016952985

Russell, Barbra E., Author
Yes! I Said No! How to Set Healthy Boundaries and Increase Your Self-Esteem
Barbra E. Russell

ISBN: 978-0-9980779-0-1

SELF-HELP / Personal Growth / Self-Esteem

QUANTITY PURCHASES: Schools, companies, professional groups, clubs, and other organizations may qualify for special terms when ordering quantities of this title. For information, email Barb@BarbraRussell.com

All rights reserved by Barbra E. Russell and Noble House Press.
This book is printed in the United States of America.

With a grateful heart I dedicate this book to the two special men in my life, my husband Jerry and my son Dane. With love and encouragement, they supported, pushed and walked alongside me in writing "Yes! I Said No!"

Table of Contents

Acknowledgments

To the wonderful people who helped me create this book:

Polly Letofsky, Bobby Haas, Victoria Wolf and My Word Publishing team who brought excellence and creativity to this book;

Friends, relatives and colleagues who encouraged and cheered me on; all those I've taught and counseled who have shared their stories and who have enriched my life as we've journeyed together.

AUTHOR'S NOTE

The examples, anecdotes, and characters in this book are drawn from my clinical work and life experience with real people and events. Names and some identifying features and details have been changed, and in some instances people or situations are composites.

Introduction...

I'VE SPENT THOUSANDS OF counseling hours working with many people who *want* to say **"No,"** who *need* to say **"No"** but who say **"Yes"** anyway!

For example, consider Bob, who had been asked to be a youth leader, a Sunday school teacher, a greeter, a deacon, and part of the leadership team at his church. He had a wife and two small children and oh, by the way, he also worked a full-time job! While he enjoyed each aspect of his involvement at church, he was beginning to feel frustrated and unappreciated. Bob needed to learn to say **"No,"** and he came to my office for help.

On Bob's first visit to my counseling office, we discussed Solution Focused Brief Therapy (SFBT), the method of treatment I typically utilize. Using SFBT meant we would not spend much time discussing his past unless that past was impacting the present. I also told him that, as a Licensed Professional Counselor with more than twenty years' experience, I could assure him that he was certainly not alone; I had worked with thousands of people through the most difficult of times. Many were people who also felt overwhelmed and stressed out; some who had even rushed to the emergency room because anxiety and panic had caused chest pain, difficulty breathing, and numbness in their arms - symptoms similar to a heart attack. Others had been referred to me by concerned friends and relatives who saw the barely-controlled anger and people's lives seemingly out of balance because they said **"Yes"** when they desperately needed to say **"No."**

Just knowing he was not alone helped a lot, Bob stated. He had always been the type of guy who could handle a lot of responsibility and juggle many balls at one time with no problem. Now, he was beginning to feel like there was something very wrong with him. He rather shamefacedly asked, "Am I going crazy? Or am I just being stupid?" I assured him the answer to both those questions was "No;" however, he did need to learn about setting boundaries. I could see a tangible change in his face and demeanor; Bob was feeling hope for the first time in a long time. Here was something he could learn; this was a problem he could tackle!

Susan was also someone who couldn't say **"No."** She came to see me because of extreme anxiety, panic attacks, and depression. Can you imagine being so anxious that you break out in hives? Can you picture feeling so depressed you want to just hide in the closet? That was Susan. She was even forced to stop working, and this strong Christian woman worried that God surely had abandoned her.

Perhaps you haven't reached that place of desperation, but if you can't say **"No,"** you will wind up feeling used, resentful, and headed for burnout. Or, like Susan, you could wind up with extreme anxiety and depression.

Let me tell you a little about Susan's road to freedom. It was sometimes lonely and often difficult, but ultimately so rewarding!

Unable to take any medication for anxiety and depression, she set out on a journey with not much more than an attitude of "I'm sick and tired of being sick and tired," the support of her loving husband, and a commitment to do what she needed to do. What Susan didn't yet realize was that her anxiety was a gift, wrapped up in a crisis. Over the years, she had adopted an unhealthy lifestyle, one of trying to please others. Now, built-up emotions of resentfulness and dissatisfaction were rising to the surface. Those emotions created a rush of adrenaline which caused her heart to start beating rapidly, precipitating the feeling of panic. Her body was crying out: "Help! Something needs to change!"

Susan came to me thinking she just needed to calm down, but after listening to a bit of her history, I realized she was carrying a lot of emotional baggage from her past. That very day, we began to work together to make changes in her life.

It took her a while, but recently Susan triumphantly declared she has learned to stand up for herself and no longer feels at the mercy of anyone who asks her for something. Now she carefully evaluates those requests, answers **"Yes"** to some and **"No"** to many. Because she no longer feels so drained, depressed and discouraged, she relishes the additional energy she enjoys, has joined a gym, lost weight, completed a 5K run, and feels excited about life!

This is certainly a different Susan than the one I met a year earlier.

Can learning to say **"No"** do all that? Absolutely! In this book, I will share the tools and skills Susan, Bob, and many others have learned, and you too can one day proudly proclaim: **"Yes! I said No!"**

One

Why Is It So Hard To Say "No?"

HAVE YOU EVER NOTICED that two-year-olds don't seem to have a problem saying **"No?"** That's one of the first words they learn!

But somewhere along the line, something happens. And that feisty little two-year-old turns into a wimpy adult who can't say **"No."** What happened?

Think of all the messages that children, teens, and young adults hear along the way: "Children should be seen and not heard." "Don't you talk back to me, young lady (or young man)!" "I'll make you sorry you argued with me!" Some messages come with a slap or a hit and *all* such messages from our parents have a powerful impact.

What children learn from their environment growing up becomes normal to them. Think about it; if children live with hostility, they learn to fight. If they live with fear, they learn to be apprehensive. If they live with criticism, they learn to be critical - of others and of themselves.

I remember talking to a grown woman whose eyes filled with tears as she stated, "I was unwanted. My mother wanted a boy." As she grew up, she believed men were better than women. No wonder she felt she had nothing to contribute. Feeling less worthy than any man led her to believe she was unworthy in general. She couldn't speak up to her mother, and later, that pattern included almost everyone.

I've talked with others who can't really put their finger on the problem; they just know that they have a hard time saying **"No."** It's easier to go along with what others want. How does this happen? Let me describe a psychological learning cycle:

1. **We stay silent to survive.** When you're a child, and you get in trouble for disagreeing with the adults, you fear you'll be thrown out and will not survive. As adults, we recognize this isn't true, but when your cognitive reasoning is not yet developed, a primal fear takes over. Sometimes, a child hides and stays silent to escape a beating. The more often that occurs, the more often a message gets buried deep within the psyche: **"Stay Silent to Survive."**

2. **Silence Becomes a Habit.** After years of learning not to speak up, this becomes a habit that you quickly adopt. The silent child becomes a non-communicative teenager, and then a constrained adult. Often, along the way, people figure out ways to compensate; they may engage in unhealthy patterns of manipulation, passive-aggressiveness, and using guilt to get their way.

3. **Habit Becomes a Lifestyle.** I have a sign in my office which reads, "If it doesn't work, do something different. If it works, do it more." If you keep doing the same thing over and over again, pretty soon that just becomes how you live - it becomes your lifestyle. By the time a habit becomes a lifestyle, the individual has discovered what works and they "do it more." If they've discovered that saying **"No"** is too hard, it's easy to slip into the known, the familiar, the accustomed - and it becomes their lifestyle.

4. **Lifestyle Becomes an Identity.** After a lifetime of not speaking up, the adult then says, "that's just who I am. I can't speak up." By that time, the habit has become a lifestyle, the lifestyle has become their identity, and that identity has become an unconscious state of being. This is not questioned until there is some significant event, a different environment, or exposure to an entirely different way of thinking.

Sometimes hidden deeper in the psyche than the psychological learning cycle is a need and desire to be included, which can mask a fear of rejection, a need for approval, or a belief that you must please others. Deeply-instilled reactions might even come from the need for physical safety - like the child who hides when a drunken parent comes home. Just as damaging, however, is the lack of emotional safety. These are the children who are ridiculed every time they offer a thought or opinion. They quickly learn not to speak up, lest they get hurt, abandoned, or not loved. **Surviving in silence produces invisibility!**

However, what helped you as a child no longer works when you grow up.

Another sign in my office reads: "Dad – A boy's first hero, a girl's first love." Too many boys and girls experience either a physically or emotionally absent father and that hunger for dad – the **hero**, the first **love** - is exceedingly strong! My relationship with my father typified a daughter's longing for love, approval, and acceptance. I didn't hear, "I love you," or "that's a great job – I'm proud of you." When there were no hugs or shows of affection, without realizing it, I began to inwardly starve. And just as the physical body begins to shrink when deprived of nutrients, my emotional and spiritual soul started to wither.

I was still a young girl when the psychological cycle kicked in.

First, out of **necessity** and a huge desire to be accepted, I began to "perform." I thought, "maybe if I do really well in school, if I'm a 'good girl' at home, at church and everywhere else, he'll tell me he loves me."

Second, my performance became **habitual**. After all, there were some pay-offs for being really, really good! I was praised when I brought home all A's and I was the center of attention when I read the entire Christmas story in the second grade. As I grew older, I enjoyed the validation received when I was the "best." Yes, I was rewarded for performing.

Third, I began to adopt a **lifestyle** of wanting to please, fearful I'd say the wrong thing. And I began to lose my own identity in the quest to become someone else.

Finally, my new identity became **"The Performer."** I couldn't find the courage to speak up, especially to older males (go figure!). I became resentful, afraid, and had no real feeling of self-worth, although I still automatically put on a good act.

When I finally gained the courage to recognize what I'd become, my counselor helped me discover the broken child within. With tears flooding down my face, I found my voice. In the safety of that counseling office, long-buried emotions came pouring out as I offered forgiveness and found acceptance.

Then something wonderful happened! I became me – the REAL ME! What joy! What excitement! Now, when I succeed in life, I celebrate. If I mess up, I may first flip out, but then I learn from it. And do you know what else? I learned to say **"No!"** What a relief, to be honest, to say **"Yes"** to what I want and **"No"** to what I don't without worrying about what people might say, or what they might think of me.

Perhaps, like me, you need someone to help you learn to say **"No,"** and to become the "Real You." I encourage you to implement the tools in this book, discover your voice, let your **"Yes"** be **"Yes"** and your **"No"** be **"No!"** As you find that person God intended you to be, you begin to live out His purpose in your life. That will definitely include being able to declare, **"Yes! I Said No!"**

Two

People Pleasing Is Not a Spiritual Gift!

ARE YOU A PEOPLE PLEASER?

A client recently said to me, "I can't help it – being a people pleaser is just my personality. I think it's my gift."

My response? "No, *People Pleasing* is not a spiritual gift. You might be an encourager or have a gift of hospitality, but a *People Pleaser* is not who you are designed to be."

Her eyes widened, and she looked at me as if I had asked her to give up her two beloved Chihuahua puppies. She was shocked! This was an entirely different way of thinking for her, as it is for many people who believe they must please others.

Where does that unhealthy belief come from? If you're always trying to please people, in general, it's because you're afraid of something. Are you afraid they won't like you? Are you afraid of conflict? What is it that you fear might happen? If you've defined yourself as a *people pleaser,* let's look at some steps to change.

Step One – Acknowledgment

Until you take ownership of your thoughts and look at the "reasons" behind them, your mind will be "frozen in fear." Once you start to imagine what *might* happen, anxiety arises and old coping patterns and beliefs kick in. You tell yourself, "I just can't do that;" "I can't help it." Such statements actually send calming chemicals to the brain, similar to the relief smokers experience with the first few puffs of nicotine. Feelings of panic and stress diminish; you've just received a "get out of jail free" card, permission to avoid the anxiety which accompanies such thoughts.

A destructive cycle then ensues - your mind relays the message: "This is what works when you feel anxious. Do it more." Like smoking that cigarette or taking a drink when you feel stressed, telling yourself "that's just who I am" becomes an addictive pattern – a way to survive, then a habit, soon a lifestyle, and finally an identity.

Since self-doubt and fear are tricks of the mind, however, the solution lies in the saying: *"you can't conquer what you don't confront."*

How do you confront? You simply declare: "I'm afraid people won't like me, so I try really hard to please them."

The good news is that once you actually admit it, a wonderful psychological principle kicks in: *once acknowledged, fear loses a lot of its power to control you!*

Step Two – Face Your Fears

Imagine what might happen if you didn't say **"Yes"** when you actually meant **"No."** I remember my first venture into this unknown territory of saying **"No."** I was angry with a friend who planned a party for her relative, then sent me a bill for my "part." She hadn't asked first, but because she had a habit of charging ahead with plans, my first thought was, "Well, that's just who she is, and I have to accept it."

I had been hoping **she** would change; **she** would apologize and say **she** was wrong. Isn't that what most of us hope for? We want *others* to change; it would be so much easier *for us.*

After further deliberation, however, I realized I was getting sick and tired of "having to accept it," and I was ready to do something about it. *I* was the one who would have to change, and to do so, I needed to *face my fears.*

I listed them as follows:
1. If I don't give her the money, she could get mad.
2. We might have an argument.
3. I might lose that friendship.

Then I evaluated each one:

1. She could get mad. Well, I was already mad, so it was ok if she got upset as well!

2. We might argue. I wouldn't like that - who enjoys conflict? Not me! However, I was ready for that to happen so things could change.

3. I might lose a friendship. That would also be sad, but I decided I didn't really want a friend who would take advantage of me.

By looking at each possible scenario, I was *facing my fears*. And at the end of the day, I recognized that even if the worst happened, I would be ok. It might be painful (growth usually is), but I was no longer frozen in fear! In fact, I felt surprisingly confident and strong.

After carefully writing down and evaluating each fear, I, too, discovered those fears were no longer quite so scary. I was able to plan what I wished to say, practice in front of my husband, and sally forth to meet my enemy - my fears! Amazingly, when I honestly stated my concerns and what I'd like to see differently in the future, my friend quickly apologized, and we were able to negotiate a new scenario. I thought it was also incredible that each one of my fears failed to materialize. She didn't get mad, we didn't have a big fight, and even more important, she is still my friend.

Another truth I came to realize then and have had emphasized again and again is that the anticipatory anxiety which rushes over us in contemplating saying **"No"** or having such discussions is almost always worse than the actual event.

I supervise several counseling interns. One of them recently reported: "As a people-pleaser, I was really afraid when I had to confront a couple about their marriage." However, he knew this was necessary and found the courage to bring it up in the counseling session.

Sure enough, the couple seemed upset. The session ended on a rather tense note, and that's when he had to *face his fears*: "What if they don't return? What if they think I'm a bad counselor? What if I *am* a bad counselor?"

However, the following week the couple did return and reported something a bit surprising to him. "You know what?" They said, "when you talked to us about what was going on in our marriage, it was hard for us to hear, but that became a turning point for us. We were forced to look at some things we hadn't dealt with before, and it changed our relationship. Our marriage is better because you confronted us."

Our young intern began to redefine his counseling and spiritual gifts – and they didn't include being a *people pleaser*.

That's generally what happens. When you don't confront in anger, are not rude but instead bring up things in a caring way, you're no longer a *people pleaser*. In fact, you become a *people helper*. And usually, the most important person you help is yourself.

It's true, *people pleasing is not a spiritual gift*. I encourage you to change that self-label. Use your true gifts, whatever they may be - in your job, in your ministry, in your community - and you will accomplish what you were created to do here on this earth.

And remember, you can *conquer what you confront!*

Three

Care Without Carrying

"*O*F COURSE, I'LL DO *that for you!*"

"*I have to help out my kids — they just keep messing up!*"

"*I better check up on things; people need me to do it the right way.*"

"*OK, I'll give you money again, but it's the last time!*"

Do any of these statements sound familiar? If so, you could be **"carrying"** people instead of **"caring"** for them.

"What's wrong with helping and doing things for people?" you may ask. "I'm just trying to be loving and selfless. Isn't that how we're supposed to act?"

Well yes, to a point. But the goal here is to help people because you feel good inside, and you have *extra* to give. When you serve out of the abundance of your heart, you've taken care of yourself; you know who you are; your confidence and self-validation is *internal*. That is to say, you don't need others to repeatedly assure you that you've done a good job or that you're worth something. You know that inside; you feel confident and good about yourself. From that knowing, you give freely.

On the other hand, people who wind up **carrying** others generally do so because they have a deep desire to feel appreciated or needed, and they don't feel that great about themselves on the inside. Have you ever known someone who has been so beaten down by the world that they're starving for some **care** themselves? I've met several people like that. John never received love from his father; Betty's attention had to be directed toward her sick mother; as the oldest child, Mary wound up taking care of her younger siblings. Hungry for words of affirmation, of acknowledgment or praise, they easily fell into routines of doing for others. And then there are those thousands of very good, caring people who believe it's their job to do more for others than they do for themselves. And so they *carry* when they should be *caring*.

To make things even more confusing, most *"carriers"* also receive gushing and grateful comments from others who say things like: "Oh, I couldn't have done that without you!" Or, "You've saved my life! You are so wonderful!"

Inevitably, however, problems arise. That <u>external</u>

validation isn't long-lasting. The "helper" usually winds up burnt out and resentful. And, the "helpee" never develops needed self-confidence and lacks resilience.

How, then, do you **care for people without carrying them?** If you've been one of these "problem solvers" who turns into a "people pleaser," it may be difficult to change what might be a lifelong habit. But it can be done.

Here are some helpful things to consider:

1. *Take ownership of your true feelings:*
    *   Feeling resentful and used are symptoms of someone who "carries" people.
    *   *"No matter how much I do, or how hard I try, people don't seem to appreciate me."*
    *   *"Lately, I feel like people are just taking advantage of me."*

Sound familiar? If it does, decide to change. Once you make that decision, you're on your way to becoming a **"caring"** person rather than one who **"carries."** As you know, you can't change what you don't confront.

When you've recognized and paid attention to your own feelings, you can start the process of looking at things a bit differently.

Think of times you've been traveling on an airplane and the safety announcement comes on. You'll hear, "If we lose cabin pressure, oxygen masks will drop down. If you're traveling with a small child, place the oxygen mask on your own face first before helping the small child."

That almost sounds counter-intuitive – we think we should take care of that small child first! But think about it, what good are you to that child if you're lying unconscious on the floor of the airplane?

Likewise, good people, caring people, often feel they must sacrifice themselves for others. They worry, fret, and stay up all night trying to come up with solutions for someone else's problem. Or they go without to give money to a relative or friend. Perhaps they change their own plans to accommodate someone else's. All these examples point to **carrying** someone, not **caring** for them.

Here are some examples of unintended, but nonetheless incapacitating, messages:

- *"You are incapable; you can't do anything without my help."*
- *"Please remain a victim so I can feel needed."*
- *"You HAVE to love me because I've done so much for you."*

These messages are like unintended sneezes when people have a virus; they're not purposeful, but they leave both the sender and receiver of the message in a drained and weakened state.

1. **Look at Your Motives:**
   - *Unsolicited advice is self-serving.* When we're telling other people how to live their lives, there's something in it for us. Why do we feel the need to "straighten them out?" Do we need to feel accepted or appreciated?
   - *Ask yourself: Is this something that person should be doing for themselves?* Are they truly capable but just willing to let someone else do the job?

2. **What should I be doing instead?**
   An important psychological principle to remember is this: **When you stop something, you need to replace that with an "instead."** Otherwise, you leave a vacuum which will quickly be filled with the same old habits.

   Become an encourager, a cheerleader. Instead of quickly agreeing to someone's request, say things like:
   - Let me think about it first.
   - I know you can do it!
   - Tell me how you're going to go about it.
   - What's the next step?
   - Look at the pros and cons.

All of these statements are ways you can demonstrate you *care without carrying*.

Four

The Power of Deciding

"Plan your day or it will slip away."
"Wishing and hoping don't get it."
"Believing others need to change won't work."

DO ANY OF THESE quotes sound familiar? They all have to do with the importance and power of *deciding*.

I trust by now you've seen the importance of saying **"Yes"** or **"No"** when it's appropriate. In Chapter Four I want to talk about being intentional, or purposefully *making a decision*. In **Yes! I Said No!** we're talking about things such as standing up for yourself. However, the principle in this chapter – *The Power of Deciding* – is one you can use in many different areas.

Two words: *"I decided"* – a short declarative sentence. So many things change in our lives when we state, *"I decided...."*

I walk without a limp because *I decided*.

I started this book because *I decided*.

I went back to school because *I decided*.

And *I decided* to declare: **Yes! I say No!** That decision, made years ago, helped me apply lessons I've learned and taught to countless others, and am now sharing with you. In all my years as a professional counselor, I have noticed the skill of saying **"No"** is one of the most needed but is still one of the least utilized. Why? I believe people are not really sure how to go about it, for one thing, and secondly, they have just delayed the decision.

We all come to that kind of decision point from different directions. Perhaps, like Susan, whom we met in the Introduction, you are "sick and tired of being sick and tired."

Maybe you've been inspired by a speaker or a book - even this one - to make changes in your life.

I think for most of us we change when we're forced to change – because indeed, change is hard! When you reach that place of frustration or resentment, and you hear yourself regularly venting, "I can't take it anymore," that's when you look for a better way.

It's also important to remember that the *decision* to change, to say **"No"** when you've been saying **"Yes"** for too long, has to be consistently practiced. We creatures of habit can sabotage ourselves by trying something a time or two, then when things don't magically change, we declare "well, that didn't work."

Remember, studies show it takes 21 days or longer to implement a new routine. And, that's when we do it differently every day. When you're learning to say **"No,"** you may have to create opportunities to practice that every day, even if it's in your mind. (Actually, practice _especially_ in your mind.)

Neuroscience teaches us that the brain has a "plasticity" to it which enables us to keep changing, even as we grow older! Contrary to old ways of thinking, we now know you _can_ "teach an old dog new tricks" because the brain is always learning how to learn, and is always changing.

The 21-day cycle of awareness, decision making, focus, and practice can actually replace negative thoughts with new, positive ones. These healthy thoughts are like "tiny new plants" which need nurturing to grow.

For example, when I said, **"I decided"** to _walk without a limp_ it was because I had endured 10 surgeries on my right leg over a 15-year span and I definitely had a pronounced limp. Muscles and tendons had been removed, arteries and veins cut and cauterized to remove rare tumors which doctors had feared would either end my life or at the very least, result in an amputated right leg.

While I was grateful to be alive and still have two legs, I wanted to _walk without a limp_. So **I made a decision**. That's when I discovered for myself that your brain can learn new patterns of thinking and of giving directions. However, it took even more than a 21-day cycle for my body to habitually maintain the steps I undertook to change:

- I needed to regularly stretch all the muscles in my body, particularly those in my legs. So I **decided** to implement a new morning routine of discipline: I told myself: "Stretching comes before the first cup of coffee."

- I practiced "heel-then-toe" walking. It was like learning to walk all over again because I had been compensating for the pain that followed each surgery. For many years I had been walking in an unnatural position and had to change such patterns.

The good news? **The Power of Deciding** was the catalyst for me. After following the steps listed above, I can now walk without a limp! That same power is yours when you **decide**!

Let me ask you two questions that relate to the **Power of Deciding.**

1. When did you make a **decision** that resulted in a change of direction for you? Perhaps you **decided** to say no to an offered cigarette or drink, and you now see that decision led to a different group of friends or a changed life. Maybe you **decided** to take a risk and move away from home, from familiar loved ones and well-established routines that made you feel safe. Or possibly you **decided** to go back to school or start your own business. Whatever those **decisions**, review them now and recognize the **power** they provided. Such evaluation will increase your faith and confidence and help you answer the second question:

2. What **decision** is in front of you now? There's an old saying which goes: "There's nothing so constant as change." If you're going to grow, you'll need to change. One of the most empowering decisions I've seen people make is when they move from being a victim of circumstances to taking charge of their lives. I well remember one of my clients, Maria, saying to me: "I can't help it; I hate what my mother says to me, but she's my mother. I can't ignore her or tell her to shut up. There's nothing I can do."

     "Yes, there is," I responded. "You just need to recognize that sometimes your decision is to do nothing. And that's ok. You may tell yourself, 'I've **decided** that I'm unwilling to make my mother unhappy at this stage of her life so I will make the most of a bad situation. But *she's* not making me decide this; **I** have decided.' Maria, that's a powerful statement!"

I also remember talking to a young wife who was wrestling with whether or not to divorce her husband. He had cheated on her, more than once, and, being a religious woman, she felt even the Bible vindicated her when it declares that divorce is justified when the spouse has been unfaithful. However, she was torn between staying in her marriage or listening to the advice of all around her who declared, "he's no good; he's lied and cheated on you. You need to divorce him." Her heartfelt cry was, "I don't have a choice! Anything I do is going to be wrong and hurt someone."

The fact of the matter was; she *did* have a choice; she just didn't like the options. If she stayed for the sake of her children, she was opening up herself for criticism from those she trusted and loved. If she divorced, they'd all approve, but she worried about the impact that **decision** would have on her family.

I told her what I had stated to Maria and to others who find themselves in such untenable positions: "You really <u>*do*</u> have a choice; you may not like it, but when you can take responsibility for *not* making a decision, you're already a step ahead."

For example, she could say: "I don't know whether I'll divorce or not, but right now, I'm doing nothing. I'm taking my time to think about it, and I'm happy with that decision."

A follow-up statement I make which is not quite so popular with my clients goes like this: "If there's something you don't like, do something about it. If you feel like you can't or don't wish to, for whatever reason, that's ok. Just recognize that it is **your decision**, and you no longer have permission to complain about the situation."

As unhappy as they generally are about such statements (we'd all rather just complain until the world changes around us!) that **decision** is very empowering - they're once more in charge of their lives. If they wish to change it at some future date, they can.

The **Power of Deciding** is in your hands!

Five

To Be Successful, Invest in Yourself

L ET'S FACE IT; MOST people associate saying **"No"** with going to the dentist and getting a root canal - it may be necessary, but they really don't want to do it. And some people have justifiable reasons for saying **"Yes"** when they really want to say **"No."** Victims of domestic violence, for example, often learn the hard way that it's not safe to speak up or disagree with an abusive partner. Most of us, however, are merely victims of bad habits, and it's easier to "just say yes."

As you've read through these chapters, I'm sure you've recognized the need to say **"No"** at the appropriate times, and you've decided to become an emotionally healthier person who does so.

How, then, do you begin?

In the following chapters, you will find specific tips and skills to help you embark on an amazing journey. While this is not an overnight trip to success, following these steps will build self-esteem, improve self-confidence, and increase understanding of "self-care."

Remember when you first learned to ride a bicycle? As you drummed up the courage to mount that two-wheeled monster, you probably had an adult who ran along beside you, helping you keep your balance and celebrating when you actually rode a few feet all by yourself. This book is like that helpful grown-up; as you apply the principles, it is here to guide and instruct you.

As you reflect on that first adventure, I'm sure you'll remember wobbly beginnings and perhaps a few falls, but you faced the "bicycle monster" and rode triumphantly away! And today, even if you haven't ridden a bicycle in years, I also know you could hop right on and take off for a ride. The skills you acquired then serve you still. It is the same with learning to say **"No."** This ability, once mastered, becomes a part of the new, healthier you.

Susan, whom you met earlier, told me about the first time she took off on her first "boundary-setting ride." She had learned about the importance of saying **"No,"** she had worked on building up her confidence, and she was ready for a trial run. She made plans with her friend Mary to go to lunch and afterward enjoy a shopping trip. However, Susan had a secret agenda. This was the day she was going to practice saying **"No."**

The time drew near. Although Susan felt much more sure of herself after some soul-searching and progress in counseling, she was still very nervous and confessed the butterflies in her stomach almost made her cancel her date. But she was determined and knew that Mary was a safe "practice person."

At lunch, she informed Mary she would be unable to go shopping with her. Susan refrained from making excuses or making up a lie as she had so many times before. She felt her anxiety rise, but she simply said, "I'm sorry, Mary. I'm going to have to cancel our shopping trip today."

"Well, I'm disappointed, of course," Mary stated, "but I understand if you can't make it today."

Susan let out a big breath. "Thank you so much! I've been learning to stand up for myself and actually say **"No"** and you helped me accomplish my goal. **"Yes! I Said No!"** Jubilantly, she began telling Mary about her new healthy self. I think this was the beginning of a beautiful friendship, one more honest than they had experienced before.

As you learn to say **"No"** it's amazing the feeling of confidence you'll experience!

Now you are ready to take the next step – begin to *Invest in Yourself*. It's been said success is knowing how to avoid being broke and stupid! Standing up for yourself and saying **"No"** definitely belongs in the "success" category. And to be successful, you must **invest in yourself.**

You've probably heard that before, but what does it really mean? If you're going to accomplish all you were meant to do, enjoy a sense of purpose and "be all you can be," you must *Invest in Yourself*.

In the following chapters, you will learn specific ways to invest in your body, your mind, and your spirit. You will also discover how to "Dream Big and Think Small," as well as set "SPAM" goals. When you implement these tools, I know you're going to enjoy a very nice return on your investment.

Six

Invest in Your Body

"Try Something New to Take Care of You"

YOUR FIRST INVESTMENT SHOULD be in taking care of your body. Well-known motivational speaker Jim Rohn once stated: "Take care of your body. It's the only place you have to live."

You don't have to look far to find diet plans, pills, and supplements which promise to make your body better than ever. Every January you will find gyms and health clubs filled to capacity with determined overweight and out-of-shape new members. Unfortunately, however, by May or June the crowds diminish and those New Year's Resolutions to have thinner, stronger, more flexible bodies are displaced by the busyness of everyday life.

"Consistency Is the Key to Change"

I have found the real key to making lasting change, whether that's taking care of your body, your mind, your finances, your career, or your relationships, is consistency. And if you're going to be consistent, you need motivation, but you also need to be realistic. Just ask those January goal-setting, purpose-driven men and women who don't make it to December.

"Two Minutes a Day"

Here's an example of something you can do for your body that requires only two minutes but reaps much more in benefits: **Deep Breathing**.

Take two minutes every morning to breathe deeply, all the way down to your abdomen. Fill your lungs with clean air, hold it, then exhale out completely. Repeat. After just a couple of minutes, you will feel the difference.

Medical research has shown some proven benefits of regular deep breathing:

- Releases toxins in your body
- Releases tension
- Relaxes mind/body and brings clarity

- Oxygenation of the brain reduces excessive anxiety
- Relieves pain
- Strengthens immune system
- Improves posture
- Strengthens the lungs and makes the heart stronger
- Helps with weight control

Wow! Do you see how a two-minute **investment** such as deep breathing pays such huge returns? Instead of sleeping late, rushing to get ready, and then rushing off to work, *try something new to take care of you.* Tell yourself, "This will only take two minutes. I can spare two minutes." Then take some deep breaths and think about all the benefits you are giving your body.

After you've *consistently* practiced deep breathing for a few weeks, you will start to feel and see the difference. Not only will your body thank you; your self-confidence will grow. When you've exercised such self-discipline, pat yourself on the back (literally and/or figuratively) and feel proud of yourself.

As you do, you'll activate some new brain-wave patterns. Because when you link an event (*breathing deeply*) with a strong emotion (*feeling proud of yourself and dancing around the room in joy*), those two get linked in your brain. The positive association creates a desire to repeat that good experience. (Think Pavlov's dogs) Fairly quickly, what you had to force yourself to accomplish through discipline will become almost automatic.

Try Something New to Take Care of You – it's just two minutes. And with those two minutes, you've started a *pathway to success!*

Seven

Invest in Your Mind

"Turn the Ship Around"

IF YOU LOOKED IN the dictionary under "angry man," you would likely see a picture of the man in my office who sat across from me. His body was tense, he wore an intense frown and with clipped words began to list all the reasons he was entitled to be angry. "I have never been appreciated," he announced. "I'm the one who's always being blamed for things not my fault." As he continued to catalog all the wrongs in his life, it was clear this man believed the world was against him.

As he told his story of a troubled childhood, failed relationships and difficulties keeping a job, I could quickly see the impact of all that negativity on his life. As a counselor, I knew he needed to feel a little bit of hope. Therefore, before we started probing into the reasons for all that anger, I acknowledged he must feel like he's all alone on a ship in the middle of a storm. However, I went on, "Even in the midst of a storm, you can *turn the ship around.*"

He quickly and loudly declared he wasn't just in a storm; he was in the middle of a tsunami. And, he wasn't so sure about *his* being able to turn anything around. He, like so many people, felt certain his circumstances were out of his control; that others should treat him differently, etc. That belief, of course, left him feeling helpless and alone. No wonder he was so angry.

I then shared some good news with him. Many years ago, the philosopher James Allen penned these words: "Order your thoughts and you will order your life. Pour the oil of tranquility upon the turbulent waters of the passions and prejudices, and the tempests of misfortune will be powerless to wreck the *ship of your soul.*" In other words, this man's life can be *transformed by the renewing of his mind.*

"Angry Man" will also surely benefit from the scriptural admonition to "… *think on things* which are true, noble, just, pure, lovely, of good report. If there is any virtue and if there is anything praiseworthy, *meditate on these things.*"

I reminded him of this ancient saying: *"As a man thinketh so is he."* As we think, we change the physical nature of our brain. Dr. Caroline Leaf, a specialist in cognitive neuroscience, said as we think we actually cause genetic expression to happen in the brain. We make proteins, and these form our thoughts. We need to realize that thoughts are real, physical things that occupy mental space in the brain.

Because I know the importance of these truths, I asked "Angry Man" to think of two or three things he might be grateful for, even now. As you might imagine, however, he struggled to come up with even one. His thoughts had for so long been ones of depression and disappointment, it was clear that changing their direction would be like *turning a big ship around* in the middle of the ocean.

While most people won't likely sink to the level of despair as "Angry Man," it is the rare person indeed who hasn't struggled to follow the principle to "renew your mind and *think on things which are true, noble, just, pure, lovely, of good report ... If there is anything praiseworthy, think on these things.*"

However, when we regularly **invest** in our minds, there are wonderful benefits. One excellent way to *renew your mind is to practice gratitude.* Interestingly, as soon as you start to feel grateful for what you already have, more good things will come your way. That's because our mindset begins to change. As we practice gratefulness, we train our brains to move in positive directions. And good things are found in positive directions.

Similar to the advantages experienced by breathing deeply for your body's benefit, let's look at the medical benefits of gratitude for your mind's benefit.

- Being grateful 15 minutes a day raises antibodies.
- Grateful people are less vulnerable to clinical depression
- Expressing appreciation instead of anger, frustration or worry improves blood and heart rate.

One woman expressed those benefits this way: "I began to put into practice the idea of saying that this would be a good day the minute I woke up. And I can positively say that I have not had a bad or upsetting day since then. The amazing thing is that my days actually haven't been any smoother or any freer from petty annoyances than they were, but they just don't seem to have the power to upset me anymore. Then every night I list all the things for which I am grateful, little things that happened during the day which added to my happiness. I know that this habit has geared my mind to pick out the nice things and forget the unpleasant ones. The fact that for six weeks I've not had a single bad day is really marvelous to me!"

I think she learned to *turn the ship around*. You can too. I challenge you to declare in the morning, "This is the day the Lord has made; I will rejoice and be glad in it. Then, at the end of the day, think of at least three good things that happened that day. You will start to feel the difference, see the difference, and you will find your mind on a different course *– you've turned the ship around.*

Eight

Invest in Your Spirit

AND NOW LAST, BUT certainly not least, I want to talk about a third area in which to invest - your **spirit**. What do you long to do? What makes your heart sing? When you **follow your dreams**, you are investing in your **spirit**.

My dream was to go back to school (after many years). I will always remember what my brother-in-law once told me: "You and Jerry (my husband) should go back to school and get your degrees."

Well, Jerry and I had worked a long time, and we felt like "we're getting too old to go back to college. What would we do with a degree now?" And we kept putting that off. Then Larry said, "Look at it this way: Four years from now, you will be four years older, but will you have anything to show for it? But, in four years if you go back to school, you will have a college degree."

That kind of stuck with me and, long story short, in spite of my doubts, in the face of my fears, I made a decision to go back to school. By making that decision, I had just made an **investment** in me, in my **spirit**. I would follow my dream.

For years I had worked in health care management, and let me tell you, I was pretty good at it. I enjoyed the work, liked the people, and frankly, I thought I'd retire in that field.

After we had gone back to school, I continued my education, received my Master's Degree in Counseling and became a Licensed Professional Counselor. Here was a *big* difference: While I *liked* the healthcare world, I absolutely *love* being a counselor. I love helping people. I love teaching and speaking from a counselor's perspective. And all because I made that investment in myself.

As with other such investments, following your dreams is often, as the old saying goes, "easier said than done."

There are many possible obstacles which can stand in your way—

- ### *Your Own Excuses*
  Others may see your potential, and you may sense it yourself, but you keep postponing taking any action. I once supervised a young intern who was not only a caring counselor but who also had a talent for speaking and writing. Her dream was to publish a book.

However, time kept passing, and although she developed several ideas, she repeatedly stated, "I'm just not good at follow-through." Her self-proclaimed limitations were stifling her potential; her own excuses were standing in her way.

- *Lack of A Support System*
  Do you know why people who join organizations such as AA or Weight Watchers experience success? They meet regularly with others who are moving toward the same goal. Such groups provide encouragement, accountability, and resources. Or, your support system might be just one person like my brother-in-law who says, "why don't you follow your dream?"

- *Your Past*
  Chaotic or dysfunctional environments, negative messages, and limiting beliefs from the past can destroy your spirit like a hungry lion pouncing on its prey. They often create self-doubt, stifle ideas and creativity, and make it hard for your **spirit** to take flight.

To overcome such barriers and begin to invest in your **spirit**, start to surround yourself with people who have succeeded in spite of difficulties. If you cannot physically meet them, invite them into your mind. I recently read the biography of Louis Zamperini, a World War II hero, former track star and Olympian whose WWII bomber crashed into the Pacific Ocean. He survived both the crash and later internment in a Japanese Prisoner of War Camp and lived a full life. After his death at age 97, the LA Times described him as "an ordinary man who did extraordinary things."

Such stories of remarkable people will inspire and motivate you. And you may not have to travel very far; you may be encouraged by listening to a family member, pastor or teacher. Jim Rohn, the motivational speaker, once said, "You are the average of the five people you spend the most time with." Who are those people in your life, and do they propel you higher?

Next, take small steps. They don't have to be big, they just have to head in the right direction. Join me in the next chapter as I discuss how to *"Dream Big and Think Small."*

Nine

Dream Big, Think Small

T O SUCCESSFULLY INVEST IN your body, your mind and your spirit, *Think Small*.

I can just hear many of you now as you exclaim "Wait a minute! I thought we were supposed to think big and have bigger-than-life dreams and a gigantic vision!" If you've read any of the ever-popular "how to succeed" books or heard many motivational speakers, that is, in fact, the message you will most often hear – *Think Big!*

That's part of the process. In fact, I believe there are **four** words which lead to success – *Dream Big; Think Small.* You must indeed have a dream which requires you to stretch, grow and get out of your comfort zone.

I once heard a wonderful statement: "The greatest achievement was at first and for a time a dream ... and dreams are the seedlings of realities." You must first spend some time visualizing, desiring and prayerfully planting dreams in your mind.

However, many people can get overwhelmed by the magnitude of a *Big Dream*. Let's say you want to start your own business. That's awesome! And it's also a *Big Dream*. You can quickly become stuck in all the thoughts, doubts, and questions which come rushing to your mind. "Do I have enough money?" "Will people actually buy what I'm selling?" "How will I plan and market?"

Often, the counseling interns I supervise want to open a private practice after graduating with their Master's Degree. As soon as they've stated their goal, however, they quickly encounter some big obstacles which appear too big, too overwhelming. They get discouraged and often stop dreaming. If they continue to procrastinate, before you know it, the vision has taken a back seat to daily living and finding a job just to make money.

So, I advise them to do what I'm encouraging you to look at here; *Think Small* - start with an action to be taken today or this week.

A good way to remember the steps involved in *Thinking Small* is to look at the acronym SPAM. Yes, looking at that can of potted meat can help you get started. Here's what the letters stand for:

S = Small and Specific
P = Practical
A = Achievable
M = Measurable

A counseling intern can use this in the following way:

S = Small & Specific: This week, I will talk to a therapist who's already established a counseling practice.

P = Practical questions include the well-known journalism questions: who, what, where, when, how?

- **Who?** Identify the counselor

- **What?** Set up an appointment to interview that person.

- **Where?** Will you take them to lunch? Or you could meet for coffee or go to the established counselor's office.

- **When?** Determine the best time to meet, as well as the amount of time he or she has available.

- **How?** Write down questions you wish to have answered – come prepared.

A = Achievable = Knowing yourself as you do, is this goal achievable? If you have something else going on this week, it's not – and you will need to come up with an alternative.

M = Measurable = At this time, you've moved beyond the "thinking" stage, and your action steps need to be measurable. You might want to enlist the help of someone to keep you accountable.

From that first week of action, an intern can set up the next goal to be achieved, step by step. The journey of a thousand steps just started, and the dream of becoming a practicing therapist is beginning to unfold!

No matter what you want to achieve, remember this:

Dream Big; Think Small and *SPAM* goals are a good way to **Invest in Yourself**. I encourage you today—be successful and make an **investment** in yourself—it'll be the best thing you ever did.

Ten

"Develop Thick, Armor-Plated Skin"

IF YOU'RE GOING TO be successful, you have to have thick skin. You know, that ability to withstand criticism and hurtful comments about who you are and what you do.

That was really brought home to me by an email I recently received:

> "Dear Barbra, I have just received a revelation of why I get depressed, and it is thrilling! While my intellect is at the college graduate level, my ability to withstand offense is very childish." The writer goes on to say, "Offenses collect on me like lint and I have buried their effects in the roots of bitterness. All the while smiling and never letting anyone know."

My writer is not the only one who is so easily hurt; I've talked to hundreds of people who feel the same way. However, if you wish to be successful, it is imperative to grow *Thick, Armor-Plated Skin.*

Emotionally thick skin becomes even more crucial as you climb the ladder to success; the higher your heights, the greater number of detractors you will have and the sharper their attacks will be.

"How do you actually develop that thick skin?" This is one of those principles which sounds amazingly true but exceedingly difficult to develop. As seems to be the case in any principle I share, I've had to learn the hard way how to apply the theory. As the e-mail writer had experienced, I too had put on a mask of confidence for years but would cry myself to sleep many nights because I worried that someone didn't approve of me or didn't like what I had said or done.

I remember the day I walked down the hall and noticed two nurses with their heads huddled together in a whispered conversation. As I grew near, they looked at me and immediately stopped talking. I, of course, just knew they were talking about me. And, I also quickly decided it wasn't good because they stopped their discussion.

For the rest of the day and into the evening and even the next day, I worried about that incident. (I obviously had not yet developed armor-plated skin.) However, that was a turning point in my self-development. I instituted two rules for myself which may help you as well:

1. **Assume the best until you know the worst.**
   Until I actually hear someone say they don't like me or hated what I had to say, I'm going to assume they like me and anything I'm doing.

2. **If you can't let some bothersome thought go within 24 hours, you must take action.**

Let's discuss those two rules a bit further:

1. **Assume the best until you know the worst:**
   I found out later the two nurses were talking about a confidential family matter – which of course had nothing to do with me. As I have discovered along the way, that's usually the case. People are not nearly as interested in us as we assume they are. I've known people to obsess over a comment like a dog worrying a bone, and they've carried offenses for months or even for years.

When you grow *thick, armor-plated skin*, you learn to let those incidents bounce off you without ruining your day. Without that protective skin, your physical, emotional and spiritual health all suffer. Indeed, medical research reveals 80-90% of illness is related to stress.

2. **If you can't let something go within 24 hours, take action.**

For me, that usually means talking to the person involved – "Hey, I'd like to talk to you about something. What did you mean when you said that?" The worst that can happen is you discover they really intended to be offensive. Usually, however, they're just being what we used to call a busy-body, trying to run your life instead of taking care of their own business. "Oh, hon, you should never wear your hair that way." "Why don't you have more kids?" "You can't even do your job right." On and on it can go.

As you begin to grow that *thick, armor-plated skin,* something interesting happens. Instead of feeling attacked, you begin to step back and think a bit more logically. Why might that person be saying something so offensive? Generally speaking, it comes from a place of insecurity or hurt. The well-known saying, "Hurt people hurt people" is really true.

You might ask yourself, "Is there any truth to what that person said?"

"Hmm, should I really get another hairstyle?" If the answer is, yes, you take *action* in that direction. If the answer is "no, I like myself the way I am," you just realize that person is coming from a place of unhealed hurts, which is their problem, not yours.

Action then takes the form of your deciding to let it go, love them anyway, and/or forgive them.

Guess what? It can happen! That same writer observed in the e-mail:

"I've seen people say hurtful things to you, and you don't seem to be bothered." If I did it, you can do it – you too can grow thick, armor-plated skin.

The bottom line to growing thick, armor-plated skin? Two rules:

Rule 1: Assume the best until you know the worst.

Rule 2: If you can't let some bothersome thought go within 24 hours, take action.

Learn to know who you are, love who you are, and never let others distract you from your purpose and goals. You've got a job to do while you're here on earth, and you need to **Grow Thick, Armor-Plated Skin** so you can do it.

We Can Be Our Own Worst Enemy!

There's another, perhaps even more important, truth related to growing thick, armor-plated skin. We need to *protect us from us!* We can be our own worst critics, thinking and often saying things like:

- "I'm not smart enough, pretty enough, fit enough, talented enough, etc. Basically, I'm not good enough."
- "It's not going to happen for me, no use in trying."

Examples of this type of thinking go all the way back to Biblical times. Moses was chosen by God for a special task—to lead the Israelites out of Egypt. And one of his first tasks was to confront Pharaoh. But Moses said, "since I speak with faltering lips, why would Pharaoh listen to me? ... O Lord, I have never been eloquent, neither in the past nor since you have spoken to your servant. I am slow of speech and tongue." Basically, he was saying: "God, I can't do that. I don't have what it takes."

But Moses had a job to do, and God wasn't going to let him talk himself out of his assignment – he needed to speak up and lead the Israelites to the Promised Land!

We, like Moses, have something to do here on earth, a purpose for our lives. And we must not let those inner voices, fears, or doubts stop us.

Lisa, a young lady in one of our counseling training classes, declared she was very shy and privately let me know that she could not speak up in class. She kept saying she had stage fright, she wasn't good with people, etc. (She probably identified with Moses!) While I respected her wishes and did not call on her, it was interesting to see what began to happen. She came to every class, sat quietly and absorbed every word.

Gradually you could see her becoming more comfortable and then one day it happened! She raised her hand and made a comment. From that day forward, she began to come out of her shell like a butterfly emerging from a cocoon. She responded to the class challenge to "step out of your comfort zone" and today, she is teaching in a foreign country, a confident, well-spoken ambassador for the USA. She has developed thick, armor-plated skin for herself.

Let me share some of the principles Lisa learned in class:

Stop Comparing Yourself with Others

Albert Einstein stated: "*Everybody is a genius. But if you judge a fish by its ability to climb a tree, it will live its whole life believing that it is stupid.*"

Steve Furtick, the author of *Crash the Chatterbox*, said the reason we struggle with insecurity is that we compare our behind-the-scenes with everyone else's highlight reel.

When you compare yourself with others, you are indeed acting as *your own worst enemy*.

Instead, celebrate you and your unique assets, abilities, strengths and gifts. Write down five of them right now to get started!

Think and speak differently

Here are three declarations I make each morning:

"This is the day the Lord has made; I will rejoice and be glad in it."

"I feel happy; I feel healthy; I feel terrific!"

"Every day in every way I'm getting better and better."

Declare your progress, not your limitations

"When I read or hear something new that will help me, I write it down and practice it as soon as I can."

"I'm developing networks in my field."

"Maybe it didn't work this time, but I'm going to keep trying."

"God, I'm going to do the best job I can do, then leave the rest to you."

When you *(1) stop comparing yourself with others, (2) think and speak differently, and (3) declare your progress, not your limitations,* you will certainly develop thick, armor-plated skin for yourself. As you do, it will change how you deal with adversity, setbacks, and discouragement. Instead of being *"your own worst enemy"* and feeling hopeless, helpless or worthless, you start becoming *"your own best cheerleader."*

Decide today that even if long ago someone made you feel "not good enough," you are determined to *meet the enemy* and *defeat him*. If Moses and Lisa can do it, so can you!!

Eleven

Myths About Saying "No"

A S WITH MOST MYTHS, saying *"No"* comes with a long history. Somehow, like your mother instructing you to always wear clean underwear in case you're in an accident, many people add *"don't say no"* to the list of truths you simply must obey! Here are some of the common myths associated with *saying "No."*

- *If I say "No" I'm selfish.*
- *When I say "No" that means I'm angry, and being angry is wrong.*
- *If I say "No" I will hurt others or be hurt by them.*
- *If I say "No" I will lose something or someone I love.*

Let's look at them one at a time:

Step One – If I say "No," I'm selfish.

Somewhere along the way the definition of "selfish" and "self-caring" got confused. Webster's Dictionary defines selfish like this: (of a person, action, or motive) lacking consideration for others; concerned chiefly with one's own personal profit or pleasure. "I joined them for selfish reasons."

Those words aren't flattering descriptions, for sure, and people don't want to be identified in those terms. And, since saying *"No"* often unconsciously gets lumped in with **being selfish**, many people won't say *"No."* However, as we have seen, saying *"Yes"* all the time when you don't mean it creates many problems.

After repeated "yesses" people can begin to feel resentful, unappreciated, and hurt. "Why doesn't someone ever do something for me?" they might ask. Very often, they push down the resulting anger, and bitterness begins to consume them. Saying *"No"* is not selfish; rather, it most often represents self Caring. When you say *"No"* when you need to, you can save and maintain relationships, preserve your own body and emotional health, as well as retain your sanity. Self-care statements sound something like this: "I won't be able to join you this time; perhaps my schedule will allow it next time." Or, "I would love to take on that project because I'm interested in the subject, but I just have too many things on my plate right now. Thank you for asking me."

Step Two – When I say "No" that means I'm angry, and being angry is wrong.

Were you taught to "turn the other cheek" when you've suffered some wrong? If you were, you're certainly not alone. Hundreds of people come into my counseling offices suffering from depression, and I find the root cause is usually buried anger, hurt, or frustration. Spoken or unspoken rules from the past dictate they should say nothing, do nothing and ignore or bury any negative emotions. They are usually surprised when I encourage them to start getting mad. But I know that acknowledging the anger and getting it out in a healthy manner is vitally important.

Often, in fact, people can use anger to motivate them to action and saying *"No"* is certainly a great way to follow this advice.

Here's an example of that principle: "I am so angry right now! I can't stand that kind of behavior, and I won't tolerate it in my home." The speaker just said *"No"* in a very healthy and productive way. And it was a good thing.

Step Three – If I say "No" I will hurt others or be hurt by them.

While some people have come to this conclusion because of the physical harm that could befall them by speaking up (such protection against physical abuse is a totally different topic), I am discussing how people deal with the emotional damage. Fear of rejection, abandonment, or betrayal looms huge in the minds of those who believe they dare not say *"No."*

I think about people I've counseled who have repeatedly been mentally beaten down by others who made demeaning comments like "you're no good," "you're so stupid," or "no one wants to hear one word of what you have to say!" Such constant and continuing verbal and emotional abuse creates a state psychology calls "low ego strength."

Low ego strength shows up in people who are not confident in their thinking, their actions, or their motives in life. Because they've been "beaten down," they've lost their ability to maintain their identity and sense of self in the face of pain, distress, or conflict. Therefore, they view challenges as something to avoid; they think and perhaps even say, "I don't have the strength to fight."

The good news about exposing this myth is that there is hope.

I remember counseling a man who felt like this. He, like others with low ego strength, was very good at his job and in other areas. You'd never guess he was suffering such pain inside. But when it came to maintaining relationships and setting boundaries, he seemed powerless to stop others from emotionally and verbally running over him. We began our work together by focusing on strengths he had and taking small steps to think, write down, and then eventually say what he wanted. It took some consistent hard work on his part to face those fears and become the person God had created him to be, but he did it.

Now, I'm pleased to tell you he has a successful marriage, a new job and church community, all because he confronted his own doubts and uncertainties. He will be the first to encourage you to knock this myth out of the ballpark. And, he will testify that saying *"No"* is a good thing.

Step Four – If I say *"No"* I will lose something or someone I love.

A small child may grow up with a parent who left, or even if parents are in the home, they are abusive or neglectful. The child wonders what he or she did wrong. After all, parents are the first ones who provide safety and comfort, love and devotion. When parents provide these things, the child feels worthwhile and develops into someone who can withstand pressure, endure crises, and bounce back. Rooted in the fears of abandonment, this myth is a powerful one indeed! If a child doesn't receive unconditional love from the most important person in that young life, there's an unconscious belief that gets built in and reinforced in the brain: "If I do something wrong, I will be thrown out, then I'll have no home, and I will surely die." The survival system in the brain kicks in and sends the message again and again: "Don't rock the boat! Say nothing! Stay silent and small!"

Teens and adults who have survived this kind of environment may be very pleasant, compliant, and likable but in general, it's because they're afraid to be any other way. As I discussed in Chapter One, it was my fear of losing the love of my father which kept me paralyzed for years and unable to say *"No."* But I discovered the truth about this myth – you can learn, grow and change from the frightened child inside to a confident adult who declares: **"Yes! I Said No!"** Even though it may be scary to look at the underlying beliefs and assumptions about ourselves and others, when we challenge those myths and look at them under the magnifying glass of truth, we find hope.

I challenge you to continue to learn, just as I hope you are doing by reading this book. As you learn new information, you become self-aware and can begin to make the necessary changes to become an emotionally healthy you.

Twelve

How to Say "No"

Without Blowing Up, Wimping Out, or Running Away

"*N*O" – A SIMPLE, two-letter word. It should be easy to say, right? "**No.**" In my experience, this small declaration of independence is often the result of a hard-fought war within the mind. Victory can be won, but the battles are tough.

Dr. John Townsend, the author of the book *Boundaries*, says that "**No**" is the Christian curse word – that's a pretty strong statement but with so many believers who "can't say no," I can see why he would say such a thing. Let me give you an example:

Remember Bob? He is the man who added multiple responsibilities to an already-full plate. He *wanted* to say

"**No**," he *needed* to say "**No**," but he said "**Yes**" anyway. As a result, he had begun to feel used and resentful; on his way to burn-out.

He, like many of us, needed to learn *how to say no without blowing up, wimping, out or running away.* What do I mean by these terms?

Blowing up – We "take it" and "take it" and "take it," until we can't "take it" anymore! Like Bob, we take on too much. From a place of resentment, we explode in anger, and usually, the relationship is blown up as well.

Wimping Out – We don't want to agree, but we also can't quite get up the courage to say "**No**." So we excuse ourselves by muttering things like: "If I don't agree, they'll be mad." "They're in a bad place right now." "They need me." "They won't like me." We can find plenty of reasons to "wimp out."

Running Away - We begin to avoid the other person, change the subject, or come up with a bunch of excuses. These are often the people who burn out and stop doing ANYTHING, going from one extreme to the other.

The question then becomes:

How do we say "No" without blowing up, wimping out, or running away?

Pass the "P's" Please

A couple of "P's" can help: <u>Planning and Practice.</u> Let's talk about Planning first:

__Planning__ – If you haven't been very good at saying, **"No,"** you will need to plan ahead and get some tools for your tool-box. Here are three:

Tool #1 – Keep It Short and Sweet

Don't explain; keep your **"No"** short and simple. Too often, people feel obliged to expound on why they need to say **"No."** However, the longer the story, the more others can find reasons why that just doesn't work. "Oh, don't worry," they'll say, "it won't take that long," "it's just for this time," etc., etc., etc.

I recently called to cancel our TV subscription. You know what that's like, right? They have specially-trained people to talk you out of canceling and often you wind up signing up again.

I was prepared this time, however, with something I call:

Tool #2 – The Broken Record Technique

Me: "I want to cancel our TV subscription."

TV Employee: "Oh, what brought you to this decision?" (ready to counter any objections I might offer)

Me: **"Broken Record"** – repeated same thing: "I just need to cancel our TV subscription."

After a couple of other efforts to get more information from me, the employee said, "Well, it's your decision. We're sorry to lose you as a customer."

Yes! I was able to say No!

Tool #3 – Learn a New Phrase – "Let Me Get Back to You."

Suppose you're asked to add something to your already full schedule, and you know you don't have time. However, you're filled with anxiety when you even contemplate "disappointing" the asker. It's important not to use this as a "wimp out;" which can drive you to say, "Sure, I'd be happy to help!" Instead, you pull out **Tool #3** and say, **"Let me check my schedule and get back to you."**

Within 24 hours, call and say, "I'm sorry; I checked my calendar, and I can't do that. I wish you all the best." If necessary, use **Tool #2 – Broken Record** – and simply repeat what you've already said. Then, pump your fist and say, **"Yes! I was able to say No!"**

Ok, you've **Planned**, and you're **Prepared**; the next step is to **Practice**. We can have very satisfying conversations in our heads that don't translate to our tongues very well. When you practice, familiarity brings comfort and confidence.

<u>**Practice**</u> using each of the tools listed above:
- In front of a mirror
- With someone else
- Writing down exactly what you want to say

Then – enjoy the freedom which comes from **Learning to Say "No" Without Blowing Up, Wimping Out, or Running Away!**

Thirteen

You've Got
A New Attitude

IF YOU WANT TO be more in charge of your own life or if there are parts of your life you want to change, I can assure you that, as the song goes, you need a *new attitude*.

And, to have a *new attitude*, you need a plan; a plan that helps you say **"No,"** that helps you set boundaries. People are usually ready to *"get a new attitude"* when they've gotten to this point: "I feel like screaming out loud! I have had enough!" They've had enough of the repeated times others have taken advantage of their time, space, money, or their good graces.

"When the student is ready, the teacher appears" is the old saying so this could be your time to declare, "I say who;

I say what; I say how much." I bet saying that would reflect *a new attitude.*

Let me teach you three steps that will help:

Step 1: Figure Out What You Don't Like

That's usually pretty easy for most of us. For example, "I don't like it when my friend asks me for rides every week, but never gives me any money for gas."

Another example might be: "I want my husband to have a real conversation with me that's not about the kids, but he never seems to have the time."

In these two instances, a pattern has been identified. Along with the pattern, most likely there are feelings of frustration, resentment, hurt, and anger. You may be surprised when I say, "If you're angry, that's good news." Often people are really angry but stuff those feelings so deeply that they wind up extremely depressed. Therefore, it's great when that anger comes roaring up like a lion from the dark cage where it's been hiding. It can give you the energy you need to take action, the first step.

However, if you stop with the first step, identifying what you don't like, you're just complaining. And instead of moving to a resolution, that generally causes more problems. You need to move to Step Two.

Step 2: Say What You Want

Sounds easy, right? But you might be surprised how hard this might actually be. Let me give you a tip - look for the opposite of what you don't like. In the first case, you want some money because you've not been receiving anything in exchange for the ride. If you don't like it when your husband is always "too busy to talk," what you want is just that - some time.

If you're worried about turning from a nice quiet person into a total jerk, an important thing to remember is you don't need to be rude or mean. But when that red flag called "resentment" starts waving, it's time to speak up. And there are good ways to find your voice.

In fact, you might want to start out with an apology. *"What?"* you might say. "I should apologize to *them*?" Yes, because you've probably not said anything. You've just been expecting the other person to read your mind. And if you did mention what you wanted a long time ago, you may not have been specific.

The combination of Steps 1 and 2 could sound like this:

Scenario One: I'd like to apologize to you because I've been feeling bad about our driving arrangement, but I didn't say anything. And I don't want anything to cause any problems in our relationship. I'd appreciate it if you could start giving me $20 a month to help with the gas bill for the car."

<u>Scenario Two:</u> "Honey, I'm sorry about something. (His ears will perk up when you say that—most men never expect to hear **that** from their wives!) I have never been clear about when I'd like for us to talk. Would you be willing to talk to me for 10 minutes after dinner before we start watching TV or doing something else?"

You will probably be amazed at the results you get when you are specific. *"Could you give me $20 a month to help with gas?" "Would you talk to me for 10 minutes?"* Otherwise, people come to their own conclusions. For instance, if you said to your husband "Can we talk?" He'd probably think: "Oh no, she wants me to **talk!** What have I done now? I'll be stuck for the next 3 hours!"

Your follow-through on the request is just as important.

<u>Scenario One:</u> "Thanks for agreeing to help with the gas money. How did you want to pay the $20?"

<u>Scenario Two:</u> "Thanks for talking to me, honey. I just needed to have someone listen to me, so that was really helpful."

Needless to say, you don't want to take advantage of either scenario by saying, "Well, I could really use $25, etc." Or, with your husband, to think "now that he's listening to me, I have some other things I want to say." Keep your word, keep your cool and make sure your *"new attitude"* is one of integrity.

Step 3: Set a Consequence

Sometimes, just clearly saying what you don't like and what you want instead will be sufficient to change things. If not, however, you go to **Step 3** – set a consequence that you can control. In other words, you say what <u>you</u> will do.

Scenario One: It's been a month, you've asked for and reminded your rider of the agreement to pay $20 a month. However, nothing other than promises is showing up. You say: "I'm sorry, but if I don't get the $20 by this Friday, I'm going to have to stop coming by to pick you up."

Scenario Two: 'Honey, we've tried for 3 weeks to have that short talk, but nothing has happened. I'd really like to develop a habit of talking, so I'm not going to prepare dinner until we've talked tonight." In both instances, you are demonstrating the integrity of keeping your word, keeping your cool and keeping that good *"new attitude."*

But First: Consider the Cost

Before you actually implement any of these steps, you need to do this: ***consider the cost.*** You ask yourself: "What might happen if I do this?"

In either scenario, you might wonder if the other person will get angry, if there might be a conflict, if your friend won't be your friend anymore, or your husband fights, sulks, or leaves.

If you are prepared to say, "even if something like that happens, I still need to do this," you're ready to go.

If you're not yet ready, you need to ask yourself the reverse question: "What might happen if I *don't* do this?" The answer is often, "I'll get angrier and could lose a friendship or even my marriage."

It's important to remember not *all* situations require taking these steps; people inevitably misunderstand things and arguments happen. And, if you've considered everything carefully, you might decide to just let some things go. When a repeated action becomes a pattern that's going to interfere with a relationship, however, you must first think about what's involved, then take the appropriate steps.

By considering the cost, you're more likely to follow through with your new resolve and enjoy the benefits of ***"having a new attitude."*** You'll also enjoy your new life and the accompanying confidence and self-control which follows.

Fourteen

Look Back to Move Forward

AFTER YOU BEGIN TO understand why it's hard to say "No" by reading the material in the first part of this book, you can then begin to incorporate the concepts, skills, and tools discussed in the later chapters.

When Susan and I recently met, we reflected on her life when she first came into my counseling office compared to now. One of the stories she related in those beginning sessions was about "The Annual Family Christmas Celebration." Per the "family rules," Susan had been unofficially designated as the hostess for these large gatherings. "You have a big house and a large yard" and "you're such a good cook" were comments which accompanied the burdens her family gratefully (and thoughtlessly) placed on her shoulders.

Her mother's expectations decreed Susan must have a fully decorated tree and Christmas ornaments in each room of her spacious house and Susan had kept up this tradition even after her mother's death.

She also prepared six to eight different types of meals for this party, as various sisters, aunts, uncles and cousins wouldn't eat certain things and preferred other dishes. So Susan labored to provide exactly what each person wanted to eat at the annual event and to have her home spotlessly cleaned and decorated, all to meet her family's expectations and demands.

As a result, Susan was totally exhausted long before the big day arrived. Her "people pleasing" kicked into high gear and she was literally a nervous wreck by the end of the holiday season.

It didn't stop there, however. Throughout the year, Susan kept trying to be "all things to all people" at work, at home, and even at church. She was literally running on adrenaline, which produced more cortisol, the stress hormone, which in turn produced more depression and anxiety. What a vicious cycle!

After many months of "just surviving," as she described it, Susan had *had enough*. The anxiety and depression were bad enough, but when she kept experiencing debilitating panic attacks, she called me. It was time to make some changes in her life. The very first time I met with her, I would have described her as the poster child, so to speak, for someone who couldn't say "**No.**"

In therapy, Susan walked through the steps in this book, session by session. First, she needed to understand why it was so hard for her to say "No" and so easily fall into "people pleasing," not only with her family but in all walks of her life.

As she increased awareness and took responsibility for problems caused by generational patterns and habits long repeated, Susan began to change, bit by bit.

For example, at a recent family Christmas gathering at her house, Susan fixed only one main meal, and other family members contributed side dishes. If someone didn't like a particular dish, she invited them to bring something they'd enjoy, adding "other people may also really like what you like."

After the New Year, I was excited to hear how things went. Susan was a bit surprised that the celebration was peaceful and enjoyable, but I wasn't. She had the knowledge and practiced the skills, and she was ready to implement them.

Of course, that success didn't guarantee every effort to set boundaries would go so smoothly. In fact, Susan described her recovery as a roller-coaster ride, with many ups and downs. Just when it seemed she would be triumphant and incorporate a new healthy practice into her routine, she would experience a let-down, a panic attack or the dreaded feeling of depression.

I explained to Susan that this is very normal; in fact, it's what usually happens. People come to therapy or read a book and decide to make changes in their lives, only to discover this same up-and-down experience. When they first start out on a journey of improvement or healing, they expect nothing but continuing improvement. Then they're shocked and dismayed when they experience a setback or have a down day. And they're usually fearful of going back to the dismal place they were before.

Many years ago, I experienced a cervical disc degeneration which caused excruciating pain, and I was bedridden for many months and unable to work for a year. The symptoms first showed up as a stiff neck, and I thought I had just slept wrong or something. But the pain continued and in fact got worse. I went to several doctors and tried various treatment options before finally finding the correct one for me.

Therefore, a year later even after I was better, if my neck got stiff, I would panic. But I had to remind myself to say: "I'm getting better, and I now know what I need to do."

Most of us have come to understand that our physical bodies require time to adjust, adapt, and change into healthier patterns of eating, exercising, and quiet time. And that's even when we are disciplined and do everything right! But since we're human, we also blow it from time to time! How many of us start a New Year's Resolution to eat only healthy foods, then grab a Snickers bar after a couple of weeks? If we keep substituting an apple a day instead of that candy bar, one day we will actually start enjoying eating in a different way!

So it goes with our emotional and mental states. If we keep substituting healthy thoughts, feelings, and actions for negative ones, they become our "new normal." But, we can also forget all the improvement we've made and get discouraged if something goes wrong.

Susan described a situation that fit this explanation exactly. She had finally been able to add activities to her calendar and agreed to babysit a neighbor's children for a week.

Although she was tired, Susan felt good about her increased workload and realized she had actually enjoyed watching the children. The following day, however, an old friend called, wanting her help, and Susan fell back into old habits. She spent a lot of time on the phone, then went rushing over to check on her friend who lived 30 miles away. The short visit turned into an overnight disaster, as Susan had to transport her friend to the hospital and stayed to be with her. Once again, she felt overwhelmed, stressed, and burnt out. "What happened?" she lamented in my office. "I had been doing so well, but the roller coaster caught up with me again."

After some additional reflection, Susan realized that, after babysitting all week, she was exhausted and not thinking clearly when her friend called. That led to a downhill spiral of people pleasing and not saying "No." Although she felt like a failure, I reminded her of the normal up-and-down pattern of recovery. She would be just fine; she simply fell off her horse, as the saying goes, and just needed to get back on.

Susan quickly decided to return to her more healthy habits. She called her friend (who had been demanding she come see her) and explained she needed some time to recover. Although not initially happy, her friend agreed and understood. They're still friends, and Susan is back on track!

We, like Susan, need to **look back to move forward**. Periodically, we need to review the progress we've made. As Susan looked back, she realized she now knows her gift is not "people pleasing." Nor did she need to carry others' burdens. With new awareness, she realized other people have lessons to learn and experiences to master, just as she did. It's better for them, and it's better for her when she "cares without carrying." It was exciting to see Susan begin to invest in herself, instead of putting others' needs before her own. By her own admission, her feelings aren't so easily hurt these days. She's developing thick, armor-plated skin! We agreed she has a new attitude and has learned to say **"No"** without blowing up, wimping out, or running away.

Susan has already started to influence others around her. Her husband recently asked her, "What did you mean by that?" His question took her by surprise because he had never asked her that before. But his tone was respectful, with a genuine "I-really-want-to-know" attitude. She quickly recovered from her surprise, and they began to discuss an earlier conversation. As they talked, both realized he had misunderstood something she had said.

It was a good thing he asked the question.

After a few minutes' discussion, the confusion was resolved. They both exclaimed, almost at the same time: "Hey! This is **way** different from what we've done before!"

That prompted Susan to inquire, "How did you think to ask me that question? It was so helpful."

"I decided I'd do things in a healthy way, too," he answered, with a wry smile, referring to her new-found skills discovered through counseling.

Change is happening at Susan's house, and I know it will continue to spread to others, as she practices and lives a new lifestyle of setting healthy boundaries and enjoying increased self-esteem.

Susan practiced the teachings in each chapter of this book. She's learned new ways to set boundaries and improve her self-esteem. You should see her now as she focuses on living her own life. She is a new, healthier Susan who is excited about life again. She regularly renews her mind; she's taking care of her body by swimming and running. And she's focusing on what she's called to do on this earth. I know she enthusiastically wants everyone to learn and grow as she has.

As I close this book, I hope that you, too, have put some of the tools into action. You may not be able to use everything all at once, but as you learn more, you will grow more and become an even better you.

I encourage you to remember you will probably experience highs and lows as you incorporate these concepts and principles. You may, in fact, fear you've not made any progress at all. But continue to take small steps and incorporate new skills into your lifestyle. As you do, you will realize your life has changed, and it all started when you decided to declare: **"Yes! I said No!"**

About the Author

IN 1994, AFTER WORK-ING for many years as an Administrator in a large multi-specialty medical clinic, Barbra returned to school and began a second career. She earned a Master's Degree in Counseling and is licensed in the state of Colorado. Since then she has spent many hours encouraging, motivating, challenging and inspiring individuals, couples, and families in her private practice. She has a Bachelor's de-gree in Business Administration which she utilized in her first career of leadership and management, working with physicians and staff in the healthcare field.

That second career prompted a move to Denver, Colo-rado, where she established a counseling division at a large church. Professionally, she supervises Master's Level coun-seling students from various universities in the area. She teaches a variety of training classes and oversees several support groups while continuing her own psychotherapy practice. She is also in demand as a keynote speaker, addressing such topics as:

How Do I Forgive?
Ministry and Marriage
Highly Effective Leadership
Three Steps to Setting Boundaries
Stress Management In A Crazy World
Finding Acceptance In Each Season of Life

In her free time, Barbra and her husband, Jerry, like to travel and get away to the mountains, where she enjoys one of her favorite hobbies, photography.

During winter, it's time to enjoy a fire, hot coffee and a good book. And, of course, she loves to write. In addition to writing *Yes! I Said No!* Barbra regularly publishes a blog: "Barb's Stories From The Couch" which can be found on her web site.

If you're interested in having Barbra speak to your group or organization, contact her at: www.barbrarussell.com